IT IS UNLAWFUL FOR ANY
PERSON TO FAIL TO RETURN
LIBRARY MATERIALS

	DATE DUE	
FEB 2 2 1983		
FEB 1 1 1996		
JUL 2 2 1986		
NOV 3 0 1987		
MAR 3 0 1988		

Plants That Eat Insects: A Look at
Carnivorous Plants

PLANTS THAT EAT INSECTS

A Look at Carnivorous Plants

PLANTS THAT EAT INSECTS

A Look at Carnivorous Plants

by Anabel Dean
illustrated by L'Enc Matte

Lerner Publications Company
Minneapolis, Minnesota

Cover photograph by O.S.F. of Bruce Coleman Incorporated

LIBRARY OF CONGRESS CATALOGING IN PUBLICATION DATA

Dean, Anabel.
  Plants that eat insects.

  SUMMARY: Describes the Venus's – flytrap, sundew,
butterwort, bladderwort, fungus, pitcher plant, and cobra
plant.

  1. Insectivorous plants—Juvenile literature. [1. Insectivorous plants] I. Matte, L'Enc. II. Title.

QK917.D4 1977   583   75-38480
ISBN 0-8225-0299-2

Published simultaneously in Canada by J. M.
Dent & Sons (Canada) Ltd., Don Mills, Ontario

Manufactured in the United States of America

International Standard Book Number: 0-8225-0299-2
Library of Congress Catalog Card Number: 75-38480

2   3   4   5   6   7   8   9   10   85   84   83   82   81   80   79   78

CONTENTS

MEAT-EATING PLANTS

On the island of Madagascar, off the east coast of Africa, the natives tell of a strange tree. This tree is an eater of meat, so they say—human meat. The person who ventures too close to this tree is seized by the tree's long branches and imprisoned. The branches wrap themselves so tightly around the victim that no matter how hard he or she struggles, the trap holds fast. Then slowly, but with great strength, the tree pulls its victim into its hollow center. There the body is digested, except for the bones, and the tree is nourished until another victim comes along.

Trees that eat human beings do not exist, of course. But there are certain kinds of plants that eat animal tissue. These plants live on insects and very small animals. They are known as *insectivorous* (in-sek-TIV-er-us)—insect-eating—or *carnivorous* (car-NIV-er-us)

—meat-eating plants. These strange plants are found all over the world and in many parts of the United States.

Insect-eating plants develop in much the same way that other green plants develop. They need air, water, and sunshine in order to grow. They also need certain minerals, especially nitrogen. Most plants get nitrogen from the soil in which they grow. But insect-eating plants are unable to do this. They grow in warm, marshy places, in soil that contains very little nitrogen. In order to survive, these plants make use of the nearest source of nitrogen—the animal tissue of insects. Through a mysterious process of nature, meat-eating plants are equipped to lure insects, to trap them, and to digest them for nourishment.

Because the nourishment supplied by insects is so necessary to the life of the plant, meals cannot be left to chance. For this reason, each plant is naturally equipped to attract insects by giving off a sweet odor. Lured by this odor, insects come to the plant and are trapped by its leaves. The traps vary in kind from plant to plant, but the basic difference is that some traps move and others do not.

Once the insects have been trapped, they must be turned into food. Meat-eating plants do not *chew* insects, of course. Instead, they digest insects in much the same way that humans digest food. The leaves of meat-eating plants are actually like tiny stomachs. After the leaves trap an insect, they begin to give off digestive juices. The juices first suffocate the insect and then gradually dissolve its body. The nitrogen, salts, and other minerals from the insect's body, now in liquid form, are absorbed by the plant, enabling it to grow.

In the following pages you will learn what the various kinds of insect-eating plants are and how they lure, trap, and digest their food. Don't be surprised if the story of carnivorous plants is one of the most unusual stories you have ever read. Unlike the story at the beginning of the chapter, this one is true.

THE VENUS'S-FLYTRAP

Even if you don't know much about meat-eating plants, you have probably heard of the Venus's-flytrap or have seen a picture of one. Of all meat-eating plants, the Venus's-flytrap is perhaps the best known.

The Venus's-flytrap grows in only one area of the United States—the marshlands near the coasts of North and South Carolina. Every spring, the plant's slender stalks push through the wet ground. Soon, small white flowers develop at the top of each stalk. From the base of each stalk, large leaves grow out in a circle. On the ends of these leaves grow smaller leaves, which are called *lobes*. The lobes look like hollow pods that have been split in half lengthwise. They are straight and hinged along one side, and open and curved along the other. Bordering the open edges are 18 stiff, pointed bristles. When the lobe is open, these bristles look like teeth in an open jaw. When the lobe is closed, the bristles interlock like fingers to seal the trap.

When the plant is waiting for insects, the lobes are open, revealing the pretty reddish color of the inside surfaces. On these surfaces, toward the outer edges, are tiny glands that give off a sweet juice something like honey. It is the odor of this honey, or nectar, that attracts insects to the Venus's-flytrap.

If an insect ventures into an open lobe to taste the

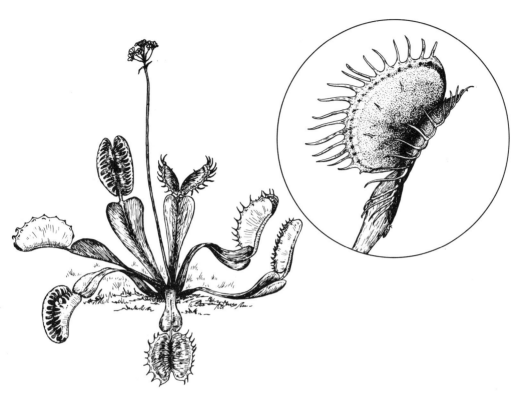

The Venus's-flytrap, with one of its traps enlarged to show details

nectar, it is in trouble. For inside, extending from both halves of the lobe, are three to four long black hairs. When touched, these hairs cause the lobe to close. Scientists are not completely certain how the hairs trigger the trap. But they believe that there is a kind of electrical current in the plant that causes the lobes to move.

If only one of the hairs is touched, the lobe will not close. The insect must touch either two hairs or one hair twice in order for the lobe to close. This is so the

1. *Attracted by a sweet odor, a fly lights on a lobe.*

2. *Once inside, it brushes against the hairs.*

3. *The lobe closes, trapping the fly.*

4. *Digestion begins and goes on for several days.*

5. *The lobe opens and the fly's skeleton drops out.*

lobe does not close when another object, such as a piece of grass, accidentally touches a hair.

As soon as the Venus's-flytrap catches an insect, digestive juices start to flow from tiny glands in the lobe. The trapped insect struggles to get out, but the more it struggles, the tighter the trap closes. The insect's struggle also makes the digestive juices flow faster. Covered by the juice, the insect eventually suffocates. The digestive juices then begin the work of dissolving the insect's body. Over a period of 8 to 10 days, the body is reduced to a soup and absorbed by the plant.

In addition to producing digestive juices, the Venus's-flytrap makes a juice that prevents the insect from decaying before it is completely digested. If part of the insect is left outside the trap, it will decay in a short time. But the trapped part will not decay before it is dissolved.

After the meal is digested, the lobe of the Venus's-flytrap opens up again. Whatever remains of the insect—usually the skeleton—is left to blow away in the wind. The lobe stays open until another insect ventures inside and is trapped. Sometimes a large insect is able to wiggle free, but most of the plant's victims cannot escape.

Each lobe of the Venus's-flytrap catches and digests about three insects before it dies. Then it withers and drops off the plant. New lobes grow and take over the work of getting food for the plant as the old lobes die.

One of the most interesting things about Venus's-flytraps is that they can tell the difference between meat and nonmeat. If you put something in the open lobe that the plant could not digest, the lobe would close as usual. But after a period of only 24 hours, it would open up again and drop the object out.

SUNDEWS

Glistening in the sunlight like a cluster of jewels is the sundew, another carnivorous plant that catches insects with a moving trap. The sundew is perhaps the loveliest of all insect-eating plants. It gets its name from the drops of juice that appear on its leaves. In the bright sunlight, these drops shine like dew.

Sundews are found in Europe, Australia, Africa, and North America. Four species of sundews grow in the United States. They thrive in swampy areas where the soil is acid and lacks nitrogen. Most sundews are small, growing to be six to eight inches tall and one or two inches in diameter. The sundews of Africa, however, grow to be three feet high. In addition to trapping insects, these plants trap small animals, such as mice.

Sundews are often hard to find, since they are usually hidden by larger plants. You can recognize sundews by their long, thin stalks, and by the flowers of pink, white, or red that bloom at the top. Toward the bottom of the stalks, growing out in a circle, are the plants' leaves. Reddish in color, they vary in shape from long and narrow to short and spoon shaped. Hundreds of sensitive hairs or tentacles cover the leaves, and each tentacle is tipped with a drop of clear, sticky juice. If you touch the juice with a toothpick, it will stretch like honey.

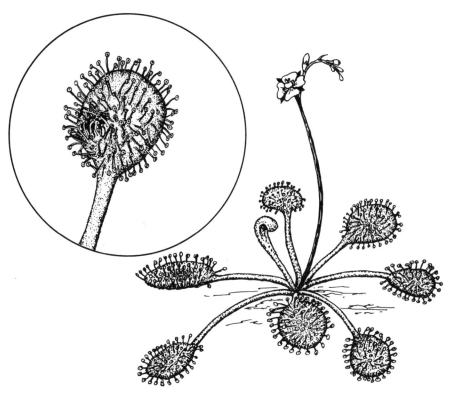

The most common variety of sundew has round leaves the size of small coins. Covering the leaves are tiny hairs tipped with sticky juice.

Insects are lured to the sundew by a sweet smell that the plant produces. When an insect ventures onto a sundew leaf, it becomes stuck in the juice. The insect struggles to get free, but the more it struggles, the more juice is produced by the plant. In a short time, the tentacles on the leaves start to bend in toward the insect. Soon the insect is hopelessly bound by the tentacles. The cells on the leaf now begin to give off

This sundew is found in Australia and South Africa. Its leaves are larger and longer than those of its American cousin. When an insect touches a leaf tip, the entire leaf curls up.

digestive juices. In a few hours, the insect is reduced to a shapeless mass.

The tentacles of the sundew leaf stay closed for four or five days, until digestion is completed. Then the tentacles uncurl and stand upright again. When the plant is ready for another meal, the sticky juice forms again on the tip of each tentacle. Each sundew leaf catches and digests about three insects before it dies. When a leaf dies, another one grows in its place. So there are always leaves to carry on the work of nourishing the plant.

Like the Venus's-flytrap, the sundew can tell the difference between food and nonfood. Only a few of its tentacles close over an object that is not meat. But when nitrogen-bearing food is placed near the plant, its leaves actually move toward it.

BUTTERWORTS

Butterworts are sometimes called bog violets because they grow in warm, marshy places and produce flowers that look like violets. The flowers are often violet in color, though they may be yellow or white as well. These flowers bloom every spring at the top of the butterwort's long stem.

The leaves of the butterwort grow in a cluster at the base of the stem. They are small leaves, with edges that curl in toward the center. Covering the leaves is a colorless substance that feels greasy to the touch. This butterlike substance is what gives the plant its name. The substance has a peculiar odor, which smells strong and musty to humans. But insects like the smell and are drawn by it.

Only the smallest insects, such as ants and gnats, are trapped by the butterwort. When an insect crawls onto a butterwort leaf, the greasy substance sticks to its body. As the insect struggles to be free of the substance, strong digestive juices start flowing from cells in the leaf. The more the insect struggles, the faster the juices flow. At the same time, the edges of the leaf start to curl together, closing over the trapped insect. In a short time, the insect suffocates.

It takes a butterwort leaf from several hours to a day to curl up completely. After the leaf has closed, it·

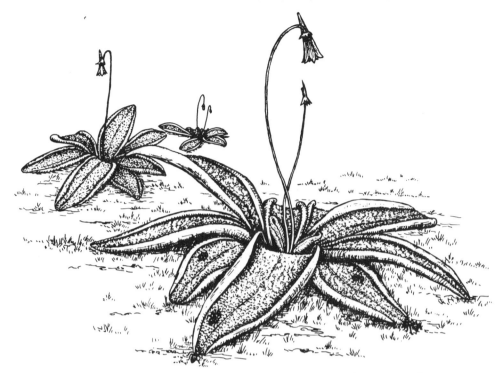

The butterwort is named for the greasy, buttery substance on its leaves. When an insect becomes trapped in this substance, the edges of the leaves curl inward and digestion begins.

remains closed for another full day while the insect inside is digested. The digestive juices reduce the insect's body to a broth. In this liquid form, minerals from the insect's body are taken into the plant through pores in the leaf. When digestion is completed, the leaf uncurls.

Of all insect-eating plants, the butterwort is the only one that is useful to human beings. The butterwort actually produces a form of antibiotic—a drug that destroys germs, or at least stops their growth. This powerful substance is present in the digestive juice of the butterwort, where its germ-killing properties prevent captured insects from decaying before they are digested. These same germ-killing properties make the plant valuable as a medicine. Many years ago, the people of Switzerland found that when they rubbed butterwort leaves directly on the sores of their cattle, the sores healed quickly. Today, many people still use butterwort leaves as a common home remedy for certain animal ailments.

Dairy farmers of the Scandinavian countries use butterwort leaves in another way. They add the leaves to crocks of milk. In a short time, the acid in the leaves curdles the milk so that it can be made into cheese.

BLADDERWORTS

Bladderworts are strange-looking plants that have no roots, only stems with hundreds of tiny balloonlike organisms attached to them. Most bladderworts live in water, but some live on land. Bladderworts are hardy plants that flourish in every part of the world, from the polar regions to the equator.

Floating in the water, the bladderwort appears to be nothing more than a long, thin stalk topped with delicate flowers. No leaves can be seen growing on the stalk. Under the water, the bladderwort's stalk trails along and branches out like the roots of a tree. On each branch, attached by small stems, are the plant's leaves. These leaves are tiny balloonlike sacs that look like bladders or bulbs. Each is an insect trap that provides nourishment for the entire plant. The bladders are so small that they can be examined only through a microscope. With the help of a microscope, a person can see the tiny trap door on each bladder and the small hairs that grow around it. These hairs trigger the trap.

To show how the trap of the bladderwort works, we must use an example. Suppose that you wanted to draw water into a small plastic bottle that had a very tiny opening. How would you go about it? You would probably squeeze the sides of the bottle together and

21

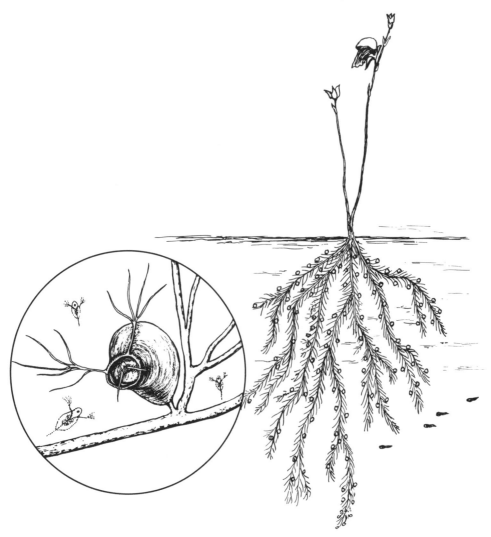

The bladderwort plant with one of its bladders greatly enlarged

then put it underwater. When you let go of the sides, suction would cause the water to rush in. The bladderwort trap works in much the same way. When waiting for a meal, the bulb is deflated (without air), so it looks flat. Soon a tiny water insect, such as a mosquito larva, comes along. Attracted by a sweet substance given off by the bladderwort, the insect approaches the plant's bulb. When the mosquito larva brushes against the hairs around the opening, the sides of the bulb suddenly expand. Water rushes into the bulb, carrying the insect with it.

Once the insect is inside, the trap door closes tight. Some of the water that has been sucked in then passes out through the walls, and digestion begins. Scientists are not sure whether digestion in the bladderwort is carried out by bacteria or by digestive juices. They do know that it takes place quickly. Most bladderworts digest small insects in 15 to 30 minutes, and large insects within 2 hours. During this time, special cells in each bladder absorb the nitrogen and other minerals from the insect's body. The hard parts of the insect remain inside the tiny bladder.

When digestion is finished, the trap door opens and the remaining water shoots out. Now the bladder is deflated again and triggered for another meal.

Bladderworts usually eat water fleas, mosquito larvae, and other tiny organisms that live in water. Sometimes the plant even catches tadpoles. When this happens, the bladder is unable to take in the entire body all at once. So it digests part of the tadpole's body first. Then it sucks the rest of the body in and digests it.

Each tiny bladder catches food about 15 times before it dies. But new bulbs are always growing to carry on the food-trapping process.

FUNGI

Fungi (FUN-jy) are simple plants that do not have stems, leaves, or flowers. They are found in many forms, ranging from microscopic organisms to molds and mushrooms. Fungi are plants that do not have the green coloring material chlorophyll in their cells. Without chlorophyll, fungi cannot make their own food. So they must live on dead or living plants or animals.

Some fungi are insect-eating plants. They are so tiny that they can be observed only through a powerful microscope. There are several varieties of insect-eating fungi, each with its own method of catching food. One variety grows tiny loops. In these loops the fungi catch microscopic worms called *nematodes*. When a nematode accidentally crawls through the loop of a fungus, it brushes against the inside of the loop. This causes the loop to suddenly tighten around the worm, trapping it. The worm struggles in the trap but finally dies. Then the fungus starts to nourish itself. Sharp points growing inside the loop pierce the worm's soft body and draw juices from it. After this is done, the fungus loop releases the worm's body, and the fungus is ready for another meal.

Like other meat-eating plants, fungi can tell the difference between what is food and what is not food.

A view of looped fungi as seen through a microscope. Trapped in the plant's loops are two nematodes, or microscopic worms.

Scientists have tried putting threads and other nonfood objects through the loops of the fungi. They have found that unless meat is placed in the loops, the loops will not tighten. The scientists believe that there is some kind of chemical reaction between the meat and the plant that causes the loops to close.

Some scientists think that nematode-eating fungi can be of help to human beings. Nematodes live in the ground and do a great deal of damage to farmers' crops. By raising more fungi, scientists hope to control the nematode pests.

PITCHER PLANTS

Common Pitcher Plant

Some insect-eating plants do not catch insects with moving traps. One that doesn't is the common pitcher plant, which is found along the Atlantic coast of North America and in many of the eastern and midwestern states. Like most other meat-eating plants, the pitcher plant grows in wet, acid soil.

The pitcher plant gets its name from its leaves, which are small pitcher-shaped containers. These leaves grow out in a circle from the base of the plant. The flowers of the pitcher plant grow high above the leaves on long slender stalks, and they vary in color from species to species. The most common species of pitcher plant has deep reddish-purple flowers.

The leaves or pitchers of each plant contain water that drowns the insects trapped inside. Most of the water is drawn up into the pitcher from the marshy soil, but some of it is also rainwater. A leafy hood growing out over the top of the pitcher limits the amount of rainwater that can fall inside. Inside the hood are tiny glands that give off a sweet juice. The odor of this juice attracts insects to the pitcher plant.

Most of the sweet juice is collected near the rim of the pitcher, but some of it runs down the outside of the plant. Insects crawl up the plant, licking the juice as

Trumpet pitcher plant

Purple (common) pitcher plant

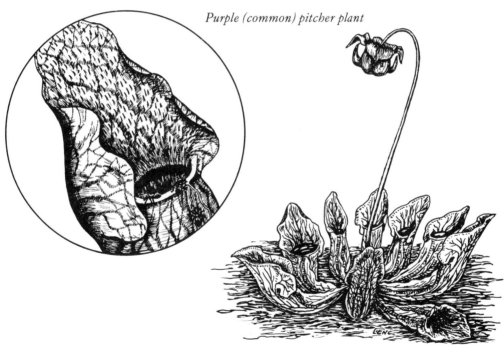

These pitcher plants represent two of the nine species that grow in North America. The plants may not look alike, but their traps work in the same way.

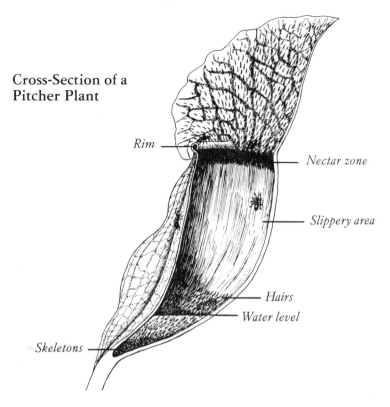

Cross-Section of a Pitcher Plant

Rim

Nectar zone

Slippery area

Hairs

Water level

Skeletons

they go. When they reach the rim, they crawl into the pitcher to get more of the juice. But inside, the plant is very slippery and the insect starts to slide down into the pitcher. Soon it comes to an area of thick hairs, all pointing downward. The insect tries to crawl back out of the pitcher, but it cannot crawl against these hairs. As the insect begins to struggle, digestive juices start to flow from the walls. The insect is washed down into the water and digested.

The pitcher walls absorb the nutritional parts of the insect. The hard, indigestible parts stay in the water at the bottom of the pitcher. With every meal, this pile grows. If you were to cut open an older pitcher plant leaf, you would find it almost filled with the indigestible parts of insect bodies.

The insects most commonly caught by the pitcher plant include ants, beetles, and flies. Flies and other winged insects are caught when they fly into the pitcher and then try to fly out again. As they fly away, they bump into the hood, fall into the water, and are digested.

Sometimes small frogs are trapped by the pitcher plant. Tree frogs, for example, like to rest inside the mouth of the plant during the day. They cling to the slippery wall by the suction pads on their feet and eat the insects that come there for the sweet juice. Once in a while, however, a frog slips into the trap and becomes a meal for the plant.

There are a few insects that are not harmed by the digestive juices inside the pitcher plant. These include certain species of flies, moths, and mosquitoes. These insects lay their eggs inside the pitcher. When the eggs hatch, the larvae feed on the insect remains in the bottom of the pitcher. The larvae are not digested by the plant because their bodies produce a protective substance. In time, the larvae bore through the sides of the pitcher and get out. While they are in the pitcher, however, the larvae are prey to birds. Birds will slit the bottom of the pitcher in order to get at the larvae.

Certain caterpillars feed on the leaves of the pitcher

plant without becoming trapped. They eat holes in the leaves and suck the sweet juices from the plant. Because they stay on the outside of the plant, the caterpillars are not in danger of being trapped.

Cobra Plant

Another species of pitcher plant grows only in northern California and southern Oregon. This is the three-foot-high cobra plant. The cobra, sometimes called the cobra lily, gets its name from the spotted hood that forms the top of the leaf. This hood gives the leaf the appearance of a hooded cobra snake, complete with fangs. The hood is also twisted, an effect that adds to its snakelike appearance. The leaves of the cobra plant are green except for the tops, which are red and yellow. The flowers of the cobra are red and white.

Like other species of pitcher plants, the cobra uses its pitcher-shaped leaves to trap insects. The opening of the cobra's pitcher is half hidden by the large hood. Just inside this opening is the sweet juice that lures insects to the plant. To reach the juice, the insects crawl up either the sides of the plant or the fanglike leaves that grow from the end of the hood. These leaves are covered with hairs to make the climb easier.

When insects enter the opening of the pitcher, they come in contact with more hairs. These hairs point

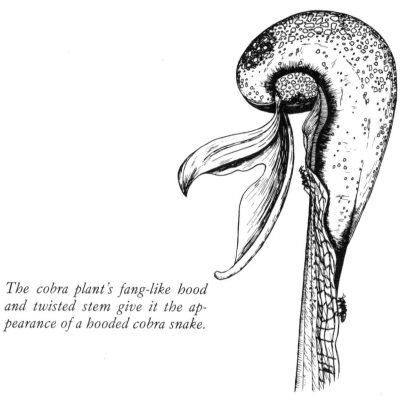

The cobra plant's fang-like hood and twisted stem give it the appearance of a hooded cobra snake.

downward, preventing the insects from crawling back through the opening. In an attempt to get out another way, the insects crawl to the spotted areas inside the hood. These spots are actually thin membranes that let in light. But the insects mistake the spots for openings, and they crawl farther into the plant to reach them. Unable to get out, the insects soon become tired and fall into the water.

Cobra plants do not give off digestive juices. Instead, bacteria in the water works on the insects' bodies. In time, the soft parts of their bodies decay. Then the useful minerals are absorbed by the plant.

31

Like other species of pitcher plants, cobra lilies have no way of getting rid of the hard remains of the insects that they catch. After a time, each pitcher collects quite a load of dead insects. These dead and decaying bodies, trapped in a large group of plants, give off an odor that can be noticed some distance away.

In addition to insects, frogs and snakes are also captured and digested by cobra plants. These animals probably crawl into the plants to eat the insects. Most larger frogs and snakes are able to get out again. But sometimes the smaller animals slide into the water and become a meal for the cobra plant.